D1064891

Inside Special Operations

NAVY SEALS

Special Operations for the U.S. Navy

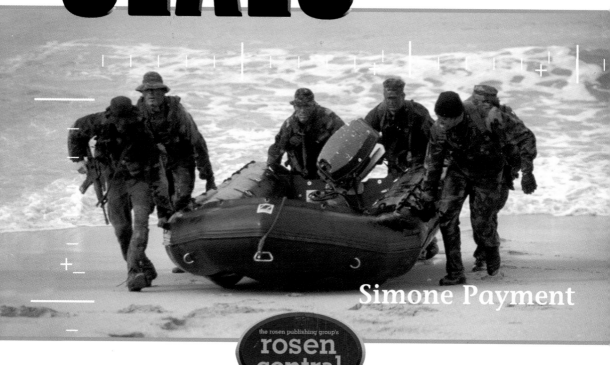

Simone Payment

the rosen publishing group's
rosen central

Published in 2003 by The Rosen Publishing Group, Inc.
29 East 21st Street, New York, NY 10010

Library of Congress Cataloging-in-Publication Data

Payment, Simone.
Navy SEALs / by Simone Payment.—1st ed.
     p. cm.—(Inside special operations)
Includes bibliographical references.
ISBN 0-8239-3809-3 (lib. bdg.)
1. United States. Navy. SEALs—Juvenile literature. 2. United States.
Navy—Commando troops—Juvenile literature.
I. Title. II. Series.
VG87 .P39 2003
359.9'84'0973—dc21

                                     2002008484

Manufactured in the United States of America

Contents

To help them operate in secrecy, U.S. Navy SEALs often wear camouflage uniforms and face paint during special missions.

Introduction

It's so dark you can't see your hand in front of your face, let alone the other men around you. You're loaded down with nearly 100 pounds of weapons, food, and equipment. It's quiet—no one says a word. Everyone walks so carefully you don't even hear footsteps. It's cold, but you need to keep moving because it will be daylight soon. You're behind enemy lines and you're in constant danger of being seen. You must move at night and sleep during the day, hidden carefully so you will not be discovered.

You're a Navy SEAL and you're on a mission. You and your SEAL team have been sent to scout an airbase. You walk for miles to reach the base, being sure not to be seen by the enemy. Once you reach the base, you make sure it is safe for the rest of the troops. Is there room for helicopters to land? Have the land mines been cleared? Are enemy soldiers hiding anywhere?

This particular mission took place in Afghanistan in November 2001. A SEAL team was sent in to prepare an airstrip for the U.S. Marines. The group was on its own. Its members had only the weapons and food that they carried. One SEAL who took part in the mission told Associated Press writer Seth Hettena: "Anything could happen. You have to be prepared."

This is just one of the many dangerous operations under-taken by the SEALs. Ever since the unit was formed more than forty years ago, SEALs have risked their lives all over the world. They are often called the "quiet professionals" because they get the job done but don't talk much about their work. Most of their missions are top secret and can't be discussed with others, not even their families. Only some 2,000 SEALs serve in the U.S. Navy. Even though they are a small group, they have a very big job.

SEALs are specially trained members of the U.S. Navy. SEAL stands for SEa, Air, and Land. SEALs are a special operations group trained to carry out missions in the water, in the air, and on the ground. However, they get specialized training in duties such as underwater demolitions and scuba diving, so most of their missions take place in or near water. Other special operations forces have their own specialties.

SEALs are highly trained and become experts at diving, demolitions, using weapons, and parachuting. They go through one of the toughest training courses in the U.S. military. Many people say that if you can make it through SEAL training, you can make it through anything. SEALs train hard because their missions are risky and require many skills. Their training has to be just as tough as what they will face in dangerous real-life situations. Some SEAL teams are specially trained for a certain type of environment, like the desert or the jungle. Those teams get extra training in the specific problems they might face in one of those settings.

"Navy SEALs have always been surrounded by . . . mystery and intrigue. [They are] the stuff of legend," writes Jason Emerson in *All Hands* magazine. They are mentally and physically tough, and they get that way by working hard. SEALs don't like to draw attention to themselves. Emerson calls SEALs "sailors whose job is to go where no one else can."

What Do 1. SEALs Do?

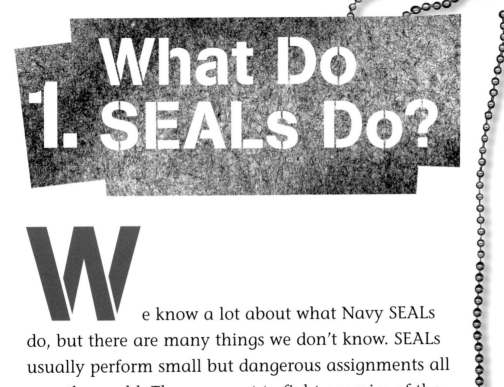

We know a lot about what Navy SEALs do, but there are many things we don't know. SEALs usually perform small but dangerous assignments all over the world. They are sent to fight enemies of the United States, criminals engaged in illegal or potentially threatening situations, and those involved in human-rights atrocities. They also protect U.S. interests. Sometimes they help fight the war against drugs. They are called on to rescue hostages on airplanes or help keep track of nuclear weapons. Some train soldiers from other countries. At times, they go into enemy lands to cut communication lines. During the Gulf War (1990–1991), for example, SEALs would sneak into enemy territory and put homing devices on buildings. Then bombs with special equipment to detect the homing devices would be dropped from planes, blowing up the buildings the SEALs had targeted.

In *U.S. Special Forces: Airborne Rangers, Delta and U.S. Navy SEALs*, Hans Halberstadt writes that most SEAL jobs are based on "stealth, shock, surprise, and precision," and we don't often hear or read about them. The SEALs and the U.S. government can't talk too much about the SEAL missions for various reasons. Pentagon spokeswoman Torie Clark said in January 2002, "We do not talk about . . . details for the obvious reasons: It puts peoples' lives at risk, and it gives the bad guys a heads-up as to what we're doing." The less the enemy understands about the SEALs, the easier it is for the SEALs to do their jobs.

The War Against Terrorism

Even though many of their assignments are secret, we do know that Navy SEALs are becoming more and more important. One of their current missions is fighting terrorism. Terrorists are "people who operate in the shadows and we have to deal with them in the shadows," U.S. defense secretary Donald Rumsfeld told the *Los Angeles Times*. SEALs are often sent on secret missions behind enemy lines. They are perfectly trained to fight the war on terrorism in Afghanistan and other countries.

When it comes to fighting terrorism, the SEALs have many types of duties. Like the mission described in this book's introduction, SEALs have gone into enemy territory ahead of other troops to make things less dangerous. They stop ships at sea to search them and make sure that terrorists are not hiding out on cargo or passenger ships. SEALs also help train soldiers in other countries to fight terrorism on their own turf.

A Recent Mission

On a mission in January 2002, some SEAL teams were sent to search tunnels at an Al Qaeda camp in eastern Afghanistan. Members of the Al Qaeda group are suspected of being involved in the terrorist attacks against the United States on September 11, 2001. The SEALs were flown in by helicopter and took enough supplies to last one day. But the operation that was supposed to take about twelve hours lasted for eight days. The SEALs found that the tunnels they were to search led to many deep caves. They realized they would need to be there much longer than the one day they had planned.

Navy SEALs were instrumental in helping to clear caves in Afghanistan following the terrorist attacks on the United States on September 11, 2001. Caves used by the terrorist network Al Qaeda and Afghanistan's former government, the Taliban, were destroyed by navy explosives experts or SEAL demolition teams.

Food and other supplies would not reach them for a few days, so the SEALs had to find, kill, and cook goats, chickens, and a cow to survive. They built a camp to try to protect themselves from freezing temperatures. The SEALs also had to protect themselves from the enemy. Enemy troops were still hiding in the hills around the camp and often shot at the SEALs.

Their mission proved successful and very important. The SEALs found many terrorist weapons and much information in the caves and tunnels. They blew up the weapons and destroyed the caves and tunnels so the terrorists could not use them again.

Other SEAL Duties

In addition to fighting terrorism, SEALs have several other types of duties. Some are called direct action. These are usually quick missions, where SEALs do things like rescue prisoners or pilots who have been shot down. These operations can also involve blowing up things like docks, bridges, or railroads. This prevents supplies from getting to enemy troops.

Other Special Operations Teams

Here are a few other special operation groups in the U.S. military. SEALs sometimes work with these groups.

U.S. Army Rangers: The Rangers scout potential battle sites before other troops arrive.

Delta Force: This is a top-secret branch of the U.S. Army. Delta Force specializes in hostage missions.

Green Berets: This branch of the U.S. Army is similar to the SEALs. Members work on secret assignments, mostly on land.

Another type of mission is called special reconnaissance. For these assignments, SEALs might sneak into enemy areas to spy and collect useful information. SEALs also have unconventional warfare missions, during which they help troops from other countries fight, usually behind enemy lines.

SEALs perform a few other jobs when they are not fighting a war. One is to train soldiers from other countries or from other branches of the U.S. military. They teach the soldiers the special skills they have learned in their SEAL training. SEALs also help develop new equipment, such as boats or guns, which they may later use in their missions. The duties that SEALs perform when they are not fighting a war help them prepare for the day when they do have to go into battle.

2. The Start of the Navy SEALs

SEALs have participated in almost every battle the United States has been involved in since their formation in 1962. But how did the SEALs get started? Before the SEALs were formed, there were groups called Naval Combat Demolition Units (NCDUs). The NCDUs were formed during World War II (1939–1945), when the U.S. Navy recognized that it needed a better way to fight the war against Japan and Germany. Those two countries often put explosives on their shores and on the shores of the countries they occupied to keep U.S.

forces from safely landing there and waging an attack. Many American troops had been killed by such explosives. The U.S. military decided to provide special training to a small group of troops who could go ashore secretly and find and destroy such explosives. This would make it safer for the other U.S. troops to attack the enemy.

In May 1944, Naval Combat Demolition Units began training at Fort Pierce in Florida. They went through training that was as difficult as it is today. They trained in the water and on land, and

The skills underwater demolition teams developed during World War II were put to good use in later conflicts. Above, frogmen train at Little Creek, Virginia, in 1947.

they learned how to operate small boats and work with explosives. By June, they were ready for their first test. The NCDUs took part in the invasion of German-occupied France. They cleared mines, steel spikes, barbed wire, and other obstacles from the beaches and coastal waters the night before the invasion. They blew up as many obstacles as they could, and the infantry was able to invade the next day, helping turn the tide of the war in Europe.

Many NCDUs were killed during their early missions because they did not have the equipment they have today. They did not even have face masks or air tanks. They had to hold their breath while swimming underwater. The NCDUs were given more training and new equipment. They were renamed Underwater Demolition Teams (UDTs). The UDTs began performing operations in the Pacific, where the war with the Japanese was still going strong. A few days before a planned attack, a UDT would swim to shore and find out what the land was like. They would make maps of the land to help the troops who were coming ashore later. The UDTs would find mines and explosives and blow them up.

These UDTs in the Pacific were very successful. They were nicknamed "frogmen" because they spent so much time in the water. After World War II, the frogmen were used in other conflicts. During the Korean War (1950–1953), the UDTs went behind enemy lines to blow up roads and bridges. This would slow down the opposing forces. It also kept guns and supplies from reaching the enemy. The UDTs also learned new skills. They began parachute training so they could jump from planes and land behind enemy lines.

The Start of the SEALs

In 1961, U.S. president John F. Kennedy realized that the conflict beginning in Vietnam was very different from others in the past. To fight in this arena, the United States would need a new kind of soldier—someone who could go into enemy territory to spy. The new soldier would need to

UDTs in the Space Program

In the 1950s, the UDTs had an interesting mission. The U.S. space program was just beginning, and many kinds of experiments were being done. UDTs took part in tests to see if men could survive in space. They also helped teach astronauts to scuba dive because being underwater is very similar to being in space. Later, UDTs were trained to help recover spacecraft when they returned to Earth. Jack Rowell, a former SEAL interviewed in *The Teams: An Oral History of the U.S. Navy SEALs*, edited by Kevin Dockery and Bill Fawcett, says they were the "first people to greet the astronauts when they splashed down on every space flight."

be able to rescue prisoners and blow up buildings and bridges. To do this, he would need special training, weapons, and equipment.

President Kennedy and the U.S. military recognized that they already had some of the necessary ingredients for success. The UDTs had special training and equipment, but they would need even more. So, in January 1962, President Kennedy formed the SEALs. The new SEAL teams had many of the same duties they have today. They destroyed enemy boats and harbors. They also rescued prisoners and spied on the enemy.

Two SEAL teams were formed. The brand-new units included some men who had been in the UDTs. They all trained in the water, becoming strong swimmers and divers. They learned demolition techniques, foreign languages, and other special skills like parachuting. The new SEAL teams took part in a few small missions in Cuba in 1962 and in the Dominican Republic in 1965. Their real test was yet to come.

The Vietnam War

Everything the early SEAL teams trained for was put to the test during the Vietnam War, which the United States joined to prevent the spread of Communism. The SEALs first went to Vietnam in 1962 to help the people of South Vietnam fight against the

North Vietnamese. They helped train the South Vietnamese and also cut radio lines and blew up bridges to keep information and supplies from reaching the north. In Vietnam, there weren't many highways or good roads. The people there did not have many cars or trucks, so they used the rivers to transport materials. The rivers were the perfect place for the SEALs to fight. All their water training was put to good use.

The SEALs planned their Vietnam missions carefully. About three weeks before a mission, they would begin studying the

Navy SEALs watch as a Viet Cong bunker in which they planted charges explodes. During the Vietnam War, SEALs worked with explosives often, but it was their water training that was put to most effective use.

enemy. They would figure out what supplies they had and what they needed. The SEALs would make sure they had the boats or helicopters they needed to take them to their target area. When they were sure they were ready, they would have a meeting to make certain everyone had the information they needed. Then the operation—an attack on the enemy or the demolition of a bridge—would be carried out.

The SEALs were very effective in Vietnam. They were allowed to do things their own way, without the rest of the military interfering too much. They didn't receive much help either. The SEALs fought in their own small teams of two to seven men. They worked at night and were effective at surprising the enemy and performing sneak attacks.

After the Vietnam War

Some Special Forces teams were shut down after the Vietnam War ended. Some military leaders believed teams like the SEALs weren't needed anymore. Others realized that Special Forces would be needed to fight small wars from time to time, in various places throughout the world.

After Vietnam, the SEALs did not have many major assignments. Then, in the 1980s, the SEALs had two missions. One was in Grenada, a small island off the coast of South America.

There, the SEALs rescued U.S. citizens trapped on the island during a civil war. The other mission was in Panama, when the SEALs prevented dictator Manuel Noriega from escaping the country. In both operations, the SEALs did the job. However, in both missions things went wrong and SEALs died or were hurt in the process.

These two missions showed that the SEALs had not obtained any real experience since Vietnam. They learned that it is difficult to stay ready to fight a war at any time. To help solve this problem, SEALs began participating in even more extensive training operations. They treated each exercise as if it were a real war.

In the 1990s, the SEALs participated in successful operations in Bosnia and Liberia. In Bosnia, the SEALs led the way for international troops to enter the country safely. In Liberia, SEALs rescued more than 2,000 people trapped by the country's civil war. These two missions showed that their increased training and planning were working. Since then, SEALs have continued to train for all kinds of assignments. They want to be ready for anything.

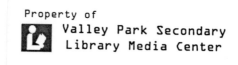

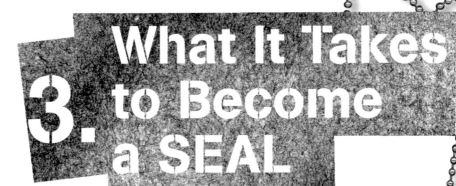

3. What It Takes to Become a SEAL

I t takes a very special person to be a SEAL. Jim Kauber, a former SEAL, described a typical SEAL in an interview with the *Los Angeles Times*. He said that SEALs are "very aggressive, intelligent, motivated, with a no-quit attitude." SEALs are risk takers, and they are driven to succeed. A Discovery Channel documentary about the SEALs claimed, "They don't have the word 'failure' in their vocabulary."

A SEAL has to be very confident, with terrific talents and skills. He has to know what he is capable of doing. To be successful, he has to know his strengths and his weaknesses.

SEALs need to be extremely physically fit and athletic. But in addition to strength and physical fitness, "one thing all SEALs have in common . . . is determination," writes Mark De Lisle, a former SEAL, in his book, *The Navy Seal Workout: The Complete Total-Body Workout*. SEALs refuse to give up; they work hard in training, on missions, and everywhere in between.

One of the aspects that sets SEALs apart from other people in the military is their intense training. To succeed in their operations, SEALs need to know how to do the job of every other man on the team. That way they can fill in for anyone who gets hurt during a mission. SEALs learn specialties like communications or weapons, but they know a lot about everyone's job. "There isn't really anything that a SEAL can't do," says Captain William M. Shepherd, a retired Navy SEAL who later became the first commander of the International Space Station, in the U.S. Navy newsletter.

Being able to work well on a team is another important characteristic for a SEAL to possess. Team members have to depend on each other at all times. When they are in dangerous situations, they need to be able to trust that the other members of the team will each do their jobs, work together, and back each other up. Captain Shepherd, explaining what teamwork is for SEALs, says, "[It] is what binds us together and sets us apart."

Requirements

To join a SEAL team, you need to be enlisted in the U.S. Navy and you need to have permission from your commanders. Before you can become a SEAL, you have to fill some basic requirements. You cannot be more than twenty-eight years old. You have to get high marks on a written exam and pass a strict physical. The physical exam includes a swim test, a one-mile run in boots and heavy pants, forty-two push-ups, fifty sit-ups, and eight pull-ups. All of these things must be done in one hour or less. Potential SEALs have to have good eyesight and can't be color-blind. The SEALs do not allow women in their ranks because the job involves ground combat. At the present time, a law prevents women from holding military jobs where they might come under fire from the enemy.

BUD/S

Although it is not easy to get into the SEAL training program, once you are accepted the real hard work begins. The unit's training program is called BUD/S. This stands for Basic Underwater Demolition/SEALs, and it is the toughest training course in the U.S. military. BUD/S lasts for seven months. Hans Halberstadt writes in *U.S. Special Forces* that it "pushes [men] to their limits of physical and emotional endurance, and beyond."

The most rigorous training course in the U.S. military, BUD/S, prepares SEALs for the challenges of real military missions. Here, recruits practice rescue tactics in a swimming pool.

On its Web site (www.navy.com), the U.S. Navy says BUD/S "prepares you for the extreme physical and mental challenges of SEAL missions." The training tries to copy situations that the SEALs will experience when they are on real missions. This way the SEALs will be prepared to face anything.

The training is very tough, but it has to be. It not only prepares the recruits for missions, but it helps the navy select the strongest and toughest recruits. BUD/S takes more than physical strength—it also takes a great deal of mental strength. Many SEAL instructors say it is impossible to predict who will make it through training. The first day you might see a big, strong man that you are sure will make it through, but that man might quit after just one week. Another recruit who might not look physically tough could have the mental toughness it takes to succeed in the program.

First Phase

After indoctrination, a five-week introduction to training, BUD/S begins. The first phase is called Basic Conditioning and lasts eight weeks. The focus of this phase is physical training.

SEAL recruits who don't complete an obstacle course on time are ordered to jump into the ocean, roll around on the beach to dry off, and run the course again.

Recruits have to swim for miles in the cold ocean. They do four-mile runs in boots and heavy clothing. Every day they are pushed to their limits. This phase is extremely tiring and difficult. Much of the time the recruits are cold, wet, and tired. Instructors like to tell the recruits that "the only easy day was yesterday."

During the first phase, recruits also have to run through a timed obstacle course. They crawl under barbed wire, climb nets, and jump from one pole to another. The recruits must finish the course in a certain amount of time and they must get faster every time they do the course. If the men don't succeed, the instructors make them jump in the ocean and dry off by rolling around in the sand. Then they have to try the obstacle course again. The obstacle course tests their "strength, agility, and speed—and mental toughness," says Hans Halberstadt in *U.S. Special Forces*. He says, "By the time you've gone through about three-fourths of it, every fiber of your muscles is burning, and you still have another quarter to go—and it's all through soft sand."

A U.S. Navy SEAL recruit walks across a suspended rope on an obstacle course during BUD/S training. In order to become a SEAL, men must complete the obstacle course in less than ten minutes.

The instructors watch the recruits carefully. They push the recruits very hard, yelling orders at them and testing their limits. The instructors train with the SEALs, so they are in top shape, too. The instructors pair up the recruits and have them train together. They learn to help each other. This is good practice for an actual mission, when they may have no one to depend on but one another.

Hell Week

The first two weeks of the first phase of training are difficult for the recruits. But the worst is yet to come. The third week of training is known as Hell Week. For five and a half days, the recruits train almost continuously. They get only about four hours of sleep the entire time.

Recruits never know what to expect during Hell Week. The instructors push trainees to the limit and beyond. Because recruits can't face combat situations during training, the instructors try to create situations that are like combat. They wear the recruits out and put them under pressure. This gives recruits an idea of what combat will be like.

"Hell Week . . . is the week that every BUD/S student must get through somehow—some way—if he wants to become a Navy SEAL," says Mark De Lisle, a former Navy SEAL. In his book, *The Navy SEAL Workout*, De Lisle writes about Hell Week: "Many times I didn't know if I would make it through . . . but each time I dug deep inside myself and found strength and determination I didn't know I possessed."

At midnight on the first day of Hell Week, instructors wake up the men by shooting blanks from an M60 machine gun. From then on, the soldiers are almost constantly on the move. They swim for hours with only short breaks. They run for miles through deep sand or

Hell Week is aptly named. Navy SEAL recruits are pushed to their physical and mental limits. Running in a group while carrying a quarter-ton log is only one of the challenges.

mud. They run in groups carrying 400–600 pound logs above their heads and do sit-ups with the log across their chests.

The recruits work around the clock. To keep up their strength, they eat a lot, but they lose weight anyway. Some throw up because they are so tired. Since they get very little sleep, many imagine that they see people who aren't really there.

Near the week's end, recruits are asked to write down why they want to become SEALs. Most are so tired that what they write doesn't make any sense. When the recruits are done with training, they get to read what they wrote. It is a reminder of how tired they were and how difficult Hell Week was.

Not everyone makes it through Hell Week, but for the recruits who do, the rest of the training is a little easier in some ways. Recruits will still have to work hard, but after enduring Hell Week, most of the time they know what to expect. Also, the instructors usually treat the recruits who have made it through Hell Week a little better. They have earned respect.

After Hell Week, first-phase training continues. More physical training exercises are held. The recruits also learn how to use

Quitting

Often during training, recruits decide they can't take any more. BUD/S is "one of the most difficult learning experiences anybody can have, and one of the things most people learn is that they don't really want to be a SEAL badly enough to finish the program," writes Hans Halberstadt in *U.S. Special Forces.* To quit BUD/S, recruits go to a certain spot on the blacktop where exercises are done. There they ring a brass ship's bell three times. Then they put the liner of their helmet on the ground near the bell and walk away.

small boats and how to make charts and maps of the water. They also develop many water skills. Recruits learn how to tie knots underwater. Eventually they are tested to see if they can tie a knot while they're fifty feet (fifteen meters) underwater. They also have to go through what is called "drownproofing." Their hands are tied behind their backs, and their ankles are tied together. They are then put in the water and have to bob up and down for thirty minutes. In another test to determine if they can survive in the water, they have to float for an hour wearing their heavy combat boots and full uniforms.

Second Phase

The recruits who make it through the first phase move on to the diving phase. This phase lasts seven weeks. The recruits continue physical training, and they must become even faster on their runs, swims, and on the obstacle course. They also spend a lot of time in the water learning how to dive. They are first trained to use diving equipment in a pool. The recruits learn what to do if the equipment doesn't work. After they are comfortable using the diving equipment in the pool, they practice diving in the ocean. The ocean training is made more difficult by the waves, the darkness, and the cold.

Training involves much more than learning how to use the equipment. The recruits also learn how to fight underwater and how to get away from the enemy.

Third Phase

During the final phase of BUD/S, recruits learn how to fight on land. They spend a total of ten weeks in this phase. For the first six weeks, they study how to work with explosives, guns, and other weapons. They learn how to find enemy explosives and how to clear mines from beaches. Instructors teach them to determine how much explosive is needed to blow up specific targets, such as bridges or boats. This is a difficult and dangerous part of training. Just like in the first phase of training, during this phase, recruits "are often cold, miserable, and tired," says Louis G. Fernbough in *All Hands* magazine. Fernbough is an instructor for this phase and says that the recruits have to think carefully when working with the explosives. "Mistakes made when working with explosives only happen once," he warns.

While the recruits are learning about explosives, they continue physical training. The requirements get tougher, and the recruits must run, swim, and do the obstacle course even faster. During this phase, recruits also practice fighting in small teams.

For the last four weeks of the third phase, recruits go to San Clemente Island to put all their skills to the test. San Clemente is an island off the coast of San Diego, California. Recruits perform many practice operations there. They plan where to put explosives; clear explosives hidden on the island by their instructors; and use all their boat and diving skills in the exercises. This training gives the recruits a good idea of what to expect once they become SEALs.

Who Makes It Through BUD/S?

Not everyone makes it through BUD/S. In fact, sometimes not even one recruit from a class graduates. In an average class, about 24 percent of the recruits who start the program make it through, according to Susan Vaughn in a *Los Angeles Times* article.

Recruits who do make it through can't always tell exactly how they did it. James C. Tipton, a former SEAL, in *The Teams* explains "[I've] never been able to tell anyone what it was that got me through it." You can prepare for the physical part of BUD/S, but "mentally, you really can't train for it," says Jim Kauber, a former Navy SEAL, in a *Los Angeles Times* article. You have to decide, "no matter what they do to me, I'm going to complete it, because it's worth it," says Kauber. "Never give yourself the option to quit," says Dennis Wilbanks, a head SEAL recruiter quoted in *All Hands* magazine. BUD/S is not easy, but many SEALs say that mental toughness and faith in oneself can go a long way toward getting through it.

4. The Next Step

After successfully completing BUD/S, recruits head to the Army Airborne School at Fort Benning, Georgia. There, they spend three weeks learning how to jump out of planes. For the first two weeks, recruits do practice drills. Finally, the third week brings what many recruits say is the fun part of training: real jumps. All recruits have to do five jumps. Some of the jumps are done when it's almost dark out, and the recruits are loaded down with heavy equipment.

Some of the jumps that the recruits learn are called HALO, which stands for high-altitude exit, low-opening. This means that the recruits jump from about 23,000 feet (7,010 meters) in the air. They free-fall for a while, before opening their parachutes close to the ground. Richard Brozack, a former SEAL, describes a HALO jump in *The Teams*. He says that when you jump, you can see for miles in every direction. Right after you jump, you continue moving almost as fast as the plane—over 280 miles (451 kilometers) per hour—before you begin to free-fall.

Another kind of jump is known as HAHO. This stands for high-altitude exit, high-opening. During a HAHO jump, recruits jump out of the plane from about 30,000 feet (9,144 meters). They open their parachutes quickly, at about 28,000 feet (8,534 meters). Then they get into formation and prepare to hit a target.

These kinds of jumps are very dangerous. At high altitudes, it is extremely cold. The temperature may be as low as –45°F (–42.7°C). At high altitudes, there is not enough oxygen in the air for the jumpers to survive. They have to breathe pure oxygen while they're in the plane. They also breathe from small canisters filled with oxygen while they are in the air. Jumpers travel faster in the thin air and may reach speeds of 180 miles (290 kilometers) per hour. If they are not careful, they can lose control. They need to be in a good position when they open their parachutes because they will immediately slow down to almost 0 miles per hour. Jumpers can get tangled in their parachutes if they are not careful. If this happens, they must

Airborne students must become comfortable jumping from planes under many different conditions. Practice jumps can only go so far, however, in preparing recruits for parachuting into enemy territory.

cut their parachute and fall to 18,000 feet (5,486 meters). Then they can open their rescue (or backup) parachute. If they find themselves in this situation, they usually do not land with the others who left the plane at the same time. In a practice jump, this is not a problem, but in a real mission, landing far away from your group can be very dangerous.

After the basic Airborne School training, recruits move on to Special Operations Technician training. This is a two-week class in secret operations given at the Naval Special Warfare

Center in Coronado, California. Next, the recruits get medical training. For more than seven months, they learn how to treat medical emergencies like gunshot wounds and burns.

First Team Assignment

After all their training, recruits are assigned to a SEAL team for six months. On their first team, they get on-the-job training and finally learn what it really means to be a SEAL. During the first six months, the recruit is on probation. This means that he has to be on his best behavior or he will be kicked off the team.

If the recruit does well during his probation, he is finally awarded the Naval Special Warfare pin. This is called the Trident, and it is something every SEAL looks forward to wearing. It is a great honor to receive the pin. The Trident is a symbol of all the recruit has accomplished.

Other Training Classes

SEALs can go to many other schools after they graduate. The Defense Language Institute in Monterey, California, is one such school. During the course of several months, the men can learn languages that will help them when they are on missions in foreign countries.

Desert Environment Survival Training (DEST) is a four-day course that teaches SEALs how to survive in the desert. They learn how to find food and water, how to build shelters to protect them from the sun, how to hide from enemies, and how to send rescue signals. After learning all these techniques, the SEALs are sent into the desert for three days to survive on their own.

Another school that teaches SEALs to survive in difficult environments is Survival Evasion Resistance Escape (SERE). At this school, the SEALs learn basic survival skills, how to avoid being captured by the enemy, and what to do if they are caught.

Leap Frogs

There is a specially chosen group of SEALs known as Leap Frogs. They are a team of parachute jumpers that perform for the public all across the United States. Fourteen jumpers leap out of a plane at 12,500 feet (3,810 meters). After free-falling to about 5,000 feet (1,524 meters), they open their parachutes and fly together to form patterns like diamonds. After their performance, they answer questions about the SEALs and sign autographs. Check http://www.sealchallenge.navy.mil/leapfrogsschedule. htm for the Leap Frogs' current performance schedule.

SEALs are never done learning. They train throughout their careers. They are always looking for new ways of doing things better, safer, and faster. SEALs participate in many training missions and exercises. In his book, *Good to Go: The Life and Times of a Decorated Member of the U.S. Navy's Elite SEAL Team Two*, Harry Constance, a former SEAL, describes a desert training exercise. His team had to sneak onto a desert missile base, blow up a missile, and then get out of the area safely. He and his team crossed the desert to the base, found the target, set up a bomb, and left. When they were far enough away, they set off the bomb. Even though this was a training exercise, they did not want to be caught, so they had to run away from the base for a few hours straight. When they finally stopped, they dug a hole in the sand. They climbed into the hole and pulled special blankets over themselves. The blankets hid them and made it impossible for their body heat to show up on special detection equipment. After sleeping during the heat of the day, the team got up at night and ran for hours. Constance writes, "Several times we ran for more than a week, covering one hundred miles [161 kilometers] or more."

Sometimes SEALs train with other military groups. Recently, SEAL Team One worked with the navy's aircraft carrier the USS *Abraham Lincoln* on a training mission. The SEALs were taken to San Clemente Island by a Sea Dragon helicopter. Dropped off in the middle of the night, they used special equipment to send pictures and information back to the aircraft carrier. During the next part of the training exercise, the SEALs rescued two pilots. Even though these missions were not real, the soldiers on the aircraft carrier and the SEALs learned how to work together.

5.Equipment

SEALs have special boats, weapons, and other equipment that make their jobs easier. Each type of equipment is specially developed to help the SEALs with their missions.

Boats

Most SEAL operations take place in or near the water, so boats are among the most important tools SEALs have. Each type of boat has a special purpose. SEALs often use patrol boats. There are several types of patrol boats, each used for a specific situation. The patrol boat, riverine (PBR)

SEAL commandos often work with SBUs (Special Boat Units). Navy SEALs use many types of boats, including the rigid inflatable boat (RIB), pictured above.

works well even in very shallow water, so it is often used in rivers. It can travel about thirty-five miles (fifty-six kilometers) per hour and is very easy to turn. The PBR can carry lots of guns and explosives. For rough water like the ocean, SEALs use patrol boat, coastal (PBC). The PBC is big, so it can handle waves and carry a lot of weapons. It is not very fast though, so it is not often used for undercover missions.

Another boat that is good in rough water is the rigid inflatable boat (RIB). The RIB was designed especially for the SEALs. It is very sturdy and will not sink even if hit by a bullet. It can carry about eight SEALs. The RIB is very light and fast. It can travel about fifty miles (eighty kilometers) per hour. The RIB works well in shallow water, so it is also good for missions on rivers.

The combat rubber raiding craft (CRRC) is so small that it can fit on a helicopter, submarine, or another boat. It can be thrown out of a plane or helicopter and then inflated on the water. It can run on motor power, or it can be rowed.

When the SEALs need to get somewhere fast but aren't too worried about being seen by the enemy, they use high-speed boats (HSBs). These boats are similar to regular speedboats.

One of the fastest boats the SEALs use is called the Mark V special operations craft. The Mark V can go nearly sixty miles (97 kilometers) per hour. It can hold about sixteen SEALs and many weapons. One of the Mark V's special features is that it is hard to detect on radar. This makes it good for secret missions.

Another vessel, the mini-armored troop carrier (MATC), is good for secret operations. It does not show up on radar and can carry lots of weapons. The MATC travels very low in the water and has a ramp at the back so the SEALs can leave the craft easily.

When the SEALs need to get to a mission from a submarine, they use an SDV. Short for swimmer delivery vehicle, the SDV is a mini-submarine. SEALs use SDVs when it is too far to swim to their targets. Each SDV can hold about eight SEALs. The SEALs get into the SDV while it is still in the larger submarine. Then the SDV is launched into the water. The SDV is filled with water so SEALs have to use scuba gear when they are inside. Also, they cannot see out of the SDV. The SEALs have to depend on special instruments to tell them where they are going.

Special Boat Units

Special Boat Units (SBUs) are also known as the Boat Guys. These navy teams are similar to SEAL teams but they specialize in using boats. They patrol rivers and harbors and help stop drug trafficking. The SBUs also work closely with SEAL teams. SBUs sometimes transport SEALs to their missions. They wait while the SEALs carry out their operations and are available to help out in case the SEALs are attacked. After the mission is complete, the SBUs get the SEALs out safely

The advance SEAL delivery system (ASDS) is another small submarine. Like the SDV, the ASDS is carried on a larger submarine. SEALs get inside and then are launched into the water. This mini-submarine stays dry inside, so SEALs do not need to use scuba equipment.

To help SEALs perform better, new equipment is often designed and manufactured for them. Many of the new vessels under development are top secret. However, an article in *New York Newsday* describes some of the new craft being worked on in the navy. One is a boat that operates underwater and on the surface of the water. Capable of traveling long distances, it can go about thirty-five miles (fifty-six kilometers) per hour above the water and eight miles (thirteen kilometers) per hour below the water. This boat is designed with more comfort in mind so the SEALs won't be as tired when they reach their missions.

Swimmer delivery vehicles, or SDVs, are launched underwater from a submarine, as shown above.

Another new vessel described in the *Newsday* article is called a swimmer transport device (STD). The STD is a "sausage-shaped, motorized sled that SEALs can drive underwater." STDs only weigh 159 pounds (72 kilograms) and can be folded up to fit into a bag.

Guns

SEALs have specialized guns to help them carry out their difficult and dangerous missions. When SEALs need to fire many bullets quickly, they use MP-4 or MP-5 submachine guns. These guns are very accurate at short ranges and are very reliable. The MP-5 works even after being in the water. Both guns are very light.

Another machine gun SEALs sometimes use is the M60. This gun can fire many bullets quickly, but it is heavier than the MP-4 or MP-5.

For targets that are farther away, SEALs use M16 rifles.

Although Navy SEALs have an extensive supply of weapons, they usually carry a handgun in case of an emergency.

A display of some of the rifles used by Navy SEALs. From top to bottom, they are the M14, the CHICOM TY56-2, a shotgun, and an M16 A with grenade launcher.

These guns are light, short, and easy to carry. They are also very accurate. The M16 has special features for SEALs, like night-vision scopes or lasers. These can show SEALs exactly where a bullet will go.

SEALs usually carry a 9 mm pistol as a backup. They can use their pistols if their main guns jam or break.

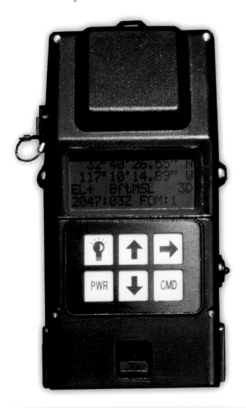

The miniature underwater global positioning system receiver (shown above) is a waterproof automatic direction finder.

Other Equipment

It is very important for SEALs to be able to communicate with each other and with their commanders. They need to be able to call for help or get information quickly. SEALs use microphones and earpieces to communicate with each other. They also use radios that send signals up to satellites and back to Earth. These radios help SEALs keep in touch with each other, even over long distances. They are easy to carry and allow SEALs to communicate anywhere in the world. A global positioning system (GPS) helps them keep track of their own positions. GPSs also help SEALs locate the sites of their missions.

6. Carrying Out Missions

SEALs have several types of missions. One is called recon, which stands for reconnaissance. In this type of operation, SEALs collect information about a potential target. They watch carefully to see how many enemy soldiers there are. They study the comings and goings of the soldiers. When the SEALs have collected a lot of information, they are ready to strike.

The SEALs have many ways to strike a target. They may send one or two men to capture an enemy soldier. Or they may send a larger group of many SEALs who quietly lay in wait and then attack.

Preparing for a Mission

Before any operation, SEALs usually have two meetings. The first is called the warning order. This meeting gives them a rough idea of what will happen on their mission. They learn what they will need to do to get ready for the assignment. They find out what gear they will need and what time they should be ready.

After the warning order, the SEALs usually get about twelve hours to prepare. SEALs spend part of this time "building their gear." They get their equipment out of the storage area and assemble it for the operation. SEALs always take good care of their equipment, but they check it extra carefully right before a mission. They need to know that everything will work properly when they are in danger on their mission. In *Good to Go*, Harry Constance describes how he prepared for his first operation in Vietnam: "I got into my tiger-striped clothes, I painted my face with green and black face paint, double-checked all my bullets, and triple-checked my gun. I checked my pistol and I checked my knife."

The second meeting the SEALs have before a mission is called the patrol leader's order. At this meeting, the SEALs get a specific plan for the operation. They get maps, photographs, or information from other soldiers. Then they are ready to go.

Navy SEALs patrolling waters on beach operations. As part of the insertion phase, SEALs often make sure waters are safe for missions.

Getting to the Mission

Sometimes SEALs get to their mission by plane or helicopter. Most of the time they travel to their operation by submarine and boat. When the SEALs are being delivered to their mission by a submarine, the sub usually stops one or two miles from shore. The SEALs put on all their scuba gear and gather their guns, explosives, and communications equipment. They get into the "escape trunk" of the sub, which is a small compartment near the exit. The SEALs close the door to the sub and then open the door to the outside. The escape trunk fills with water as the SEALs swim out into the water.

Usually one or two SEALs swim out before everyone else. They swim to the surface and inflate the small boat that the SEAL team will use to get ashore. When they have the boat ready, they swim back down and bang on the outside of the sub. This lets the other SEALs know it is time to go.

Once all the SEALs are in the small boat, they paddle quietly to shore. When they are close to shore, two divers usually leave the boat and swim closer. They watch care-fully to make sure it is safe for all the SEALs to go ashore. If it is safe, they give the signal to the other men that they can come ashore. Because they usually have to remain silent during missions, the SEALs communicate with each other using hand and arm signals. When all the men are on shore, they hide their boat and the operation begins.

Members of the Mission

Each SEAL has a specific job to do on a mission. The man in charge of an operation is called the platoon leader. Such men go through even more training than the others. The platoon leader gives orders to the SEALs on his team. He knows what each of his men can do and what they can't. He tries to keep the SEALs safe, even though he has to put them in danger on their missions.

SEALs search brush-covered terrain with MP5 9 mm submachine guns.

A point man signals to the rest of his patrol. He is indicating that he sees an enemy officer.

The point man of the mission is the first SEAL to go into any dangerous situation. He is expert at seeing in the dark. He can spot the enemy and other dangers. He looks slowly around him as he leads the way. Moving one foot at a time, he does his best to keep the rest of the team safe.

The tail gunner is the last man in line on missions. He looks out for danger behind the team, making sure no one is sneaking up on the rest of the team. SEALs often say that the tail gunner needs eyes in the back of his head.

All members of a SEAL team are always prepared for any situation. In his book, *Combat Swimmer: Memoirs of a Navy SEAL*, Captain Robert A. Gormly, a former SEAL, explains what SEALs call "lock and load." He says that it means "get ready to fire." "But," he says, "lock and load is more than that; it's a mind-set . . . [Y]ou have to be ready to go into combat at a moment's notice." SEALs are ready to face any danger, at any time.

SEALs will do whatever it takes to get the job done. Training hard, working together, and operating in secret, the SEALs are one of the most effective and valuable groups in the U.S. military.

Glossary

agility The ability to move quickly.

airstrip A runway where planes can land.

altitude Distance above the earth.

combat swimming Fighting an enemy underwater.

demolition Destruction of something, usually with explosives.

documentary A movie or television program that presents actual footage or facts about a particular topic.

enemy lines A border that separates your land from your opponent's land in a war.

global positioning system (GPS) A system of satellites that provides precise locations.

indoctrination A period of general training.

invasion The entrance of an army into a country or region during war.

land mines Explosives that are buried underground.

missile A weapon that is launched from a distance.

reconnaissance The exploring of enemy territory to get information.

recruit A new member of the military.

satellites Objects that circle Earth; used for navigation, weather study, and other purposes.

scuba Equipment used to breath underwater (stands for self-contained underwater breathing apparatus).

terrorism Using violence to instill fear to achieve a goal.

unconventional warfare Unusual ways of fighting a war.

For More Information

UDT-SEAL Association
P.O. Box 5365
Virginia Beach, VA 23471
e-mail: udtseal@infi.net
Web site: http://www.udt-seal.org

UDT-SEAL Museum Association, Inc.
3300 North A1A
Fort Pierce, FL 34949-8520
(561) 595-5845
Web site: http://www.navysealteams.com/options.htm

Web Sites
Due to the changing nature of Internet links, the Rosen
Publishing Group, Inc., has developed an online list of Web
sites related to the subject of this book. This site is updated
regularly. Please use this link to access the list:

http://www.rosenlinks.com/iso/nase/

For Further Reading

Burgan, Michael. *U.S. Navy Special Forces: SEAL Teams.* Mankato, MN: Capstone Books, 2000.

Burgan, Michael. *U.S. Navy Special Forces: Special Boat Units.* Mankato, MN: Capstone Books, 2000.

De Lisle, Mark. *The Navy SEAL Workout: The Complete Total-Body Workout.* Chicago, IL: Contemporary Books, 1998.

Streissguth, Tom. *U.S. Navy SEALs.* Mankato, MN: Capstone Press, 1996.

Bibliography

Ansarov, Aaron. "Surviving the Sand." *All Hands*, July 2001.

Constance, Harry, and Randall Fuerst. *Good to Go: The Life and Times of a Decorated Member of the U.S. Navy's Elite SEAL Team Two*. New York: William Morrow, 1997.

De Lisle, Mark. *The Navy SEAL Workout: The Complete Total-Body Workout*. Chicago, IL: Contemporary Books, 1998.

Dockery, Kevin, and Bill Fawcett, eds. *The Teams: An Oral History of the U.S. Navy SEALs*. New York: William Morrow, 1998.

Emerson, Jason. "A Legend Built on Sweat." *All Hands*, May 1998.

Garamone, Jim. "U.S. Casts Dragnet to Snag Al Qaeda, Taliban Leaders." *American Forces Press Service*, January 3, 2002.

Gormly, Captain Robert A., USN (Ret.). *Combat Swimmer: Memoirs of a Navy SEAL*. New York: Dutton, 1998.

Landau, Alan M., Frieda W. Landau, Terry Griswold, D. M. Giangreco, and Hans Halberstadt. *U.S. Special Forces: Airborne Rangers, Delta and U.S. Navy SEALs.* Osceola, WI: MBI Publishing Company, 1999.

Mazzetti, Mark, and Philip Smucker. "On the Ground." *U.S. News & World Report*, February 25, 2002.

Sanders, Edmund. "After the Attack: Battle Plans." *Los Angeles Times*, September 23, 2001.

Vaughn, Susan. "Career Make-Over: Navy SEAL Hopeful Immerses Himself in Preparations." *Los Angeles Times*, February 11, 2001.

Wilkie, Kimberly L. "Survival Evasion Resistance Escape: Learning Now Means Surviving Later." *Flight Jacket*, February 18, 2000.

Index

About the Author

Simone Payment has a degree in psychology from Cornell University and a master's degree in elementary education from Wheelock College. She has taught elementary school, worked in book publishing, and worked for a health care company. She is also the author of a biography of the Negro league baseball star Buck Leonard, a biography of the French explorer La Salle, and a book about travel careers.

Photo Credits

Cover, pp. 1, 45, 53, 54 © Hans Halberstadt/Military Stock Photo; pp. 4, 25, 26, 29 © Leif Skoogfors/Corbis; pp. 11, 19, 36 © AP/Wide World Photos; pp. 12, 27, 30, 42, 46, 47, 48 © James A. Sugar/Corbis; p. 15 © Corbis; p. 51 © Robert Genat/Zone Five Photo.

Acknowledgments

The author would like to thank Howard Cooper, Lori Cooper, and Marina Lang for their valuable suggestions and continued support.

Editor

Christine Poolos

Design and Layout

Les Kanturek